whisky cocktails

50 classic mixes for every occasion,
shown in over 100 stunning photographs

Stuart Walton

LORENZ BOOKS

This edition is published by Lorenz Books
an imprint of Anness Publishing Ltd
Hermes House, 88–89 Blackfriars Road, London SE1 8HA
tel. 020 7401 2077; fax 020 7633 9499
www.lorenzbooks.com; www.annesspublishing.com

If you like the images in this book and would
like to investigate using them for publishing,
promotions or advertising, please visit our website
www.practicalpictures.com for more information.

UK agent: The Manning Partnership Ltd; tel. 01225 478444;
fax 01225 478440; sales@manning-partnership.co.uk
UK distributor: Grantham Book Services Ltd; tel. 01476 541080;
fax 01476 541061; orders@gbs.tbs-ltd.co.uk
North American agent/distributor: National Book Network;
tel. 301 459 3366; fax 301 429 5746; www.nbnbooks.com
Australian agent/distributor: Pan Macmillan Australia;
tel. 1300 135 113; fax 1300 135 103;
customer.service@macmillan.com.au
New Zealand agent/distributor: David Bateman Ltd;
tel. (09) 415 7664; fax (09) 415 8892

Publisher: Joanna Lorenz
Senior Editor: Felicity Forster
Photographers: Frank Adam, Steve Baxter
    and Janine Hosegood
Designer: Ian Sandom
Production Controller: Claire Rae

© Anness Publishing Ltd 2008

A CIP catalogue record for this book
is available from the British Library.

Material in this book has been
previously published in *The Complete
Guide to Cocktails and Drinks*

ETHICAL TRADING POLICY
At Anness Publishing we believe that business should be
conducted in an ethical and ecologically sustainable way,
with respect for the environment and a proper regard to
the replacement of the natural resources we employ.

As a publisher, we use a lot of wood pulp to make high-quality
paper for printing, and that wood commonly comes from spruce
trees. We are therefore currently growing more than 750,000 trees
in three Scottish forest plantations: Berrymoss (130 hectares/
320 acres), West Touxhill (125 hectares/305 acres) and Deveron
Forest (75 hectares/185 acres). The forests we manage contain
more than 3.5 times the number of trees employed each year in
making paper for the books we manufacture.

Because of this ongoing ecological investment programme, you, as
our customer, can have the pleasure and reassurance of knowing
that a tree is being cultivated on your behalf to naturally replace
the materials used to make the book you are holding.

Our forestry programme is run in accordance with the UK
Woodland Assurance Scheme (UKWAS) and will be certified by
the internationally recognized Forest Stewardship Council (FSC).
The FSC is a non-government organization dedicated to promoting
responsible management of the world's forests. Certification
ensures forests are managed in an environmentally sustainable and
socially responsible way. For further information about this scheme,
go to www.annesspublishing.com/trees.

NOTES
Bracketed terms are intended for American readers.

For all recipes, quantities are given in both metric and imperial
measures and, where appropriate, in standard cups and spoons.
Follow one set of measures, but not a mixture, because they are
not interchangeable.

Standard spoon and bar measures are level.
1 tsp = 5ml, 1 tbsp = 15ml

American readers should note that the mixer known as Club soda
is referred to throughout as soda or soda water.

Front cover shows Rocky Mountain – for recipe, see page 52.

Contents

Introduction

One of the world's leading spirits, whisky (or whiskey, depending on where it hails from) boasts a distinguished history. Like the classic brandies of France, its spread around the world from its first home – the Scottish Highlands – has been a true testament to the genius of its conception. Tennessee sour mash may bear about as much relation in taste to single malt Scotch as Spanish brandy does to cognac, but the fact that they are all great products demonstrates the versatility of each basic formula.

Today, whiskies are produced all over the world. As the name is not a geographically specific one, all products may legitimately call themselves whisk(e)y. The five major producing countries are Scotland, the United States, Ireland, Canada and Japan. The name "whisky" is a variant of the phrase "water of life". In translation, the Latin *aqua vitae* became *uisge beatha* in the Scots branch of Gaelic and *usquebaugh* in the Irish.

Whisky can be used as the base ingredient for many classic cocktail recipes. It can be tricky to use, however, because its flavour doesn't take to being mixed with liqueurs and fruit juices quite as obligingly as the other spirits. The rich, sweetly woody flavours of American whiskeys, such as bourbon and rye, and the fruitiness of Canadian whisky, are better in this respect than Scotch. It is the iodiney pungency of much single malt Scotch that gets in the way. Some people may prefer drinking whisky on its own, or with nothing more elaborate than fresh spring water. Whichever way you prefer it, there is most certainly a place for whisky in every bartender's repertoire.

This book contains a tempting array of whisky cocktails, from classic drinks such as Whisky and Water, Whisky on the Rocks and Whisky and Soda, to extravagant concoctions such as the Artists' Special, Pink Almond and Irish Chocolate Velvet. Try them wisely, and have fun.

Right: Whisky can be enjoyed as the base for some delicious drinks. Each type has its own unique flavour.

What is whisky?

Historically, in countries that lacked the warm climate for producing fermented drinks from grapes, beer made from grain was always the staple brew and, just as brandy was the obvious first distillate in southern Europe, so malted grains provided the starting point for domestic production further north. Unlike brandy, however, which starts life as wine, whisky doesn't have to be made from something that would be recognizable as beer.

SCOTLAND

Home distillation in Scotland can be traced back to the 15th century, when the practice of distilling surplus grain to make a potent drink for clan chieftains was established. Initially, the drink was valued for its medicinal powers, and early examples were no doubt infusions of herbs and berries rather than the pure grain product we know today.

Types of Scotch

The most highly prized of Scotch whiskies are the single malts, which are produced entirely from malted barley, double-distilled, and made at a single one (hence the terminology) of Scotland's 100 or so working distilleries. Some of these products are aged for many

Left: Laphroaig is one of the richest of the peaty styles of Scotch produced in Islay. This Glenlivet is a ten-year-old Speyside malt from the Scottish Highlands. Whyte & Mackay whisky is re-blended for a second period of maturation.

Right: Glenmorangie is one of the most celebrated Northern Highland malts. The Famous Grouse is one of the leading brands of blended Scotch whisky. J&B is a blended whisky that is popular in the American market; J&B stands for Justerini & Brooks.

years. Twenty-five-year-old Scotch will be shot through with all sorts of profoundly complex flavours and perfumes, from the cask and perhaps from the sea air that wafts around the coastal distilleries.

Some malts are the blended produce of several single malts, in which case they are known as vatted malts. Whiskies made from corn or unmalted barley are known as grain whiskies, and are always considerably lighter in style than malts. They could be described as beginner's Scotch, since they have far fewer of the aromatic components that account for the pedigree of great malt, although they should not be seen as worthless imitations.

Blended Scotch is made from a mixture of malt and grain spirits. This is the market-leading category, occupied by virtually all of the big brand names, such as Bell's, J&B,

Johnnie Walker, Ballantine's, Whyte & Mackay, The Famous Grouse, White Horse and Teacher's. Most of these have fairly low concentrations of malt in the blend, although Teacher's and Johnnie Walker's Black Label are notable exceptions.

Scotch whisky is mostly retailed at the standard dark spirit strength of 40% ABV. A small proportion of the best grades are bottled from the barrel undiluted. These are known

as "cask-strength" whiskies. You are not intended to drink them neat, but they should be diluted with water to the level of potency you prefer.

Areas of production

For the purpose of whisky production, Scotland is divided into four broad regions: the Lowlands; Campbeltown; Islay and the Western Isles, including Jura, Mull and Skye; and the expansive Highlands region.

Lowland whiskies are generally the gentlest and sweetest styles of Scotch, while Campbeltown's are fresh and ozoney. Islay produces an instantly recognizable pungent spirit, full of seaweed and peat, while many Highland malts have a soft smokiness to them.

How it is made

In the case of malts, the grains of barley are soaked in water to encourage them to germinate. Soon after they have begun sprouting, the process is arrested by heating them in a kiln, in which variable quantities of peat will be added

Left: Johnnie Walker's Black Label has a higher malt content than the red. White Horse has a pronounced peatiness, marking the flavour of this blended whisky.

to the fuel, depending on the intended final flavour of the whisky. After kilning, the grain is mashed and drained and then poured into large tanks to begin fermentation, either with natural or cultured yeasts. The resulting brew is double-distilled in the traditional copper pot still.

The other factor in determining the character of a whisky is the maturation vessel. Scotch was traditionally aged in casks that had previously been used for shipping sherry, and some still is, but used bourbon casks from Kentucky are now quite common. In both cases, the wood is American oak, capable of imparting great richness to a whisky.

IRELAND

The origins of distillation in the Emerald Isle are lost in swathes of Irish mist, but are certainly of great antiquity. Irish whiskey once enjoyed an unrivalled reputation as a more approachable style of spirit than Scotch. It was only when blended Scotch began to be made on any significant scale towards the end of the 19th century that Irish whiskey was overshadowed.

The mellowness of Irish whiskey derives from its production process. No peat is used in the kilns, and Irish distillers use a mixture of malted and unmalted grain in their mash. It was a blended product long before today's standard Scotch blends were invented. It is then triple-distilled in a copper pot still,

which results in a product with a softer palate that still retains all its complexity. The whiskey must then be cask-aged for a minimum of three years, although in practice most varieties are aged for two to three times longer. It is usually bottled at 40% ABV.

Left: Paddy whiskey is distilled at Midleton, just outside the city of Cork in Ireland.

The brand leader on the export markets is Jameson's. Others include Bushmills, John Power, Murphy's, Paddy, Dunphy's and Tullamore Dew. All but one are made in the Irish Republic, the exception being Bushmills, which is made in County Antrim in the North.

UNITED STATES

In North America, where whiskey is mostly spelled with an "e" as it is in Ireland, production of the drink dates back to the 18th century, in the era leading up to Independence.

The first American whiskeys were made with malted barley and rye. Soon, however, a group of distillers in Bourbon County, Kentucky, began producing pure corn whiskey. By happy chance, from 1794 onwards, their communities

Left: Wild Turkey bourbon, which is aged in cask for eight years, comes from Lawrenceburg, Kentucky.

Right: In Maker's Mark, small-volume production is allied to top quality. Jim Beam is a very popular bourbon.

were infiltrated by droves of tax refugees who were fleeing from revenue officers in Pennsylvania. Suddenly, the Kentuckians had a ready-made new market for their own product and, before too long, bourbon had established an illustrious reputation.

Bourbon

Nowadays, most bourbon distilleries are concentrated not in Bourbon County, but around the towns of Louisville, Bardstown and Frankfort. Whiskeys from Kentucky are the only ones allowed to use the state name, alongside "bourbon", on the label.

Bourbon is not a straight corn whiskey, but is made from a mixture of not less than 51% corn with malted barley. Some may contain a little rye. The chief distinguishing taste of bourbon, however, derives from the barrels it matures in. These are made of new American oak, charred on the insides, which allows the spirit freer access to the vanillin and tannins in the wood.

There are two styles of bourbon: sweet mash and sour mash. The differences arise at the fermentation stage. For sweet mash, the yeasts are allowed to perform their work over a couple of days, while for sour mash, some yeast from the preceding batch augments the brew. This doubles the length of the fermentation and ensures that more of the sugars in the grain are consumed.

Most bourbon is labelled "Kentucky Straight Bourbon", which means it is made from at least 51% corn and is aged for a minimum of two years in charred new barrels. The leading brand is Jim Beam, made at Bardstown. Other brands include Wild Turkey, Evan Williams, Early Times, Old Grand-Dad and Maker's Mark.

Tennessee whiskey

South of Kentucky, in Tennessee, a different but equally distinctive style of whiskey is made. Tennessee sour mash is represented by just two distilleries – Jack Daniel's in Lynchburg, and George Dickel in Tullahoma.

Whereas bourbon is matured in charred barrels, Tennessee takes the principle a stage further by actually filtering the newly-made spirit through a mass of charcoal. In the yards behind the distilleries, they burn great stacks of sugar maple down to ash, and then grind it all to

Left: Jack Daniel's is by far the bigger brand of the two Tennessee whiskeys.

powder. This is piled to a depth of around three metres or ten feet into so-called mellowing vats.

The whiskey drips at a painfully slow rate from a gridwork of copper pipes above the vats, filtering gradually through the charcoal bed, prior to its period of cask maturation.

Jack Daniel's is one of the world's best-loved whiskey brands, led by its flagship Old No. 7 in the famous square bottle. Dickel (which spells its product "whisky" in the Scottish way), matures its No. 12 brand for several years longer, and the results are evident in a mellower nose and deeper colour. It is bottled at 45% ABV.

Southern Comfort

The foremost American liqueur is Southern Comfort. Naturally, American whiskey is used as its starting point. The exact composition of Southern Comfort is of course a closely guarded secret, but what we do know is that the fruit flavouring it contains is peach, a fruit that grows in great quantities in the southern states.

The origins of Southern Comfort probably lie in the mixing of bourbon with peach juice as a traditional cocktail in the southern

Right: Southern Comfort is a fruity whiskey liqueur of the Deep South.

states. Down in Louisiana, close to New Orleans (as the song goes), there was once a mixed drink called Sazerac. It consists of a shot of rye whiskey, with a sprinkling of peach bitters, a lump of sugar and a dash of absinthe. So traditional is it that a New Orleans company has been producing a pre-mixed version of it since around the middle of the 19th century.

The Southern Comfort distillery is located in St Louis, Missouri. The drink comes in two strengths, 40% and 50% ABV, both of which have an appealing, fruity roundness of flavour and a mellow finish.

Southern Comfort makes a good substitute for bourbon, poured over the traditional light fruitcake at Thanksgiving or Christmas. Quantities should be extremely generous.

CANADA

Whiskies from Canada are made from blends of different grains, combining rye, corn and malted barley. They nearly always contain some spirit that is produced entirely from the heavier-tasting rye, but it usually accounts for less than a tenth of the final blend. As a result, they have the reputation of being among the lightest classic whiskies of all.

Distillation is by the continuous process, in gigantic column stills. Different spirits produced from

Above: Crown Royal is a Canadian brand owned by Seagram's.

different mashes, or fermented from different yeast strains, are painstakingly blended by the distiller. All whiskies must spend at least three years in new barrels, but some are aged for 10, 12, even 18 years. The standard blends are sold at 40% ABV, but speciality aged bottlings may be stronger.

A curiosity of Canadian whisky is that the regulations permit the addition of a tiny quantity of other products, such as sherry or wine made from grapes or other fruits. While this may only account for 1% of the finished product, it makes its presence felt in the fleeting suggestion of fruitiness in some whiskies.

Most of the Canadian distilleries are situated in the eastern provinces of Ontario and Quebec. The leading label is Hiram Walker's Canadian Club, first blended in the 1880s, and is supported by the Burke's and Wiser's ranges from Corby's, McGuinness's Silk Tassel, Alberta Springs and Seagram's Crown Royal.

JAPAN

Of the leading five producers, Japan has by far the youngest whisky industry. The first distillery was established in 1923, and it is

Right: Suntory's 12-year-old Yamazaki is a kind of Japanese single malt.

only in the last 30 years or so that its products have become known elsewhere.

The model for Japan's whiskies is single malt Scotch. They are made from a mash of malted barley, dried in kilns fired with a little peat. Distillation is by the pot still method. Some of the brands are aged in used sherry or bourbon casks, and others in heavily charred new American oak. The premium brands are generally bottled at around 43% ABV.

The giant drinks company Suntory is the biggest producer of Japanese whisky, accounting for 75 per cent of the country's output. Behind Suntory comes the Nikka company, followed by the smaller producers Sanraku Ocean and Seagram's.

Cocktail-making equipment

To become a successful bartender, you will need a few essential pieces of equipment. The most vital and flamboyant is the cocktail shaker, but what you can find in the kitchen can usually stand in for the rest.

Cocktail shaker

The shaker is used for drinks that need good mixing but don't have to be crystal-clear. Once the ingredients have been thoroughly amalgamated in the presence of

Above: Measure or "jigger"

Left: Cocktail shaker

ice, the temperature clouds up the drink. Cocktail shakers are usually made of stainless steel, but can also be silver, hard plastic or tough glass. The Boston shaker is made of two cup-type containers that fit over each other, one normally made of glass, the other of metal. The Boston type is often preferred by professional bartenders. For beginners, the classic three-piece shaker is easier to handle, with its base to hold the ice and liquids, a top fitted with a built-in strainer and a tight-fitting cap. Make sure you hold on to that cap while you are shaking. As a rough rule, the drink is ready when the shaker has become almost too painfully cold to hold, which is generally not more than around 15–20 seconds.

Measure or "jigger"

Cocktail shakers usually come with a standard measure – known in American parlance as a "jigger" – for apportioning out the ingredients. This is usually a single-piece double cup, with one side a whole measure

Above: Measuring jug and spoons

and the other a half. Once you have established the capacity of the two sides, you will save a great deal of bother.

Measuring jug and spoons

If you don't have a jigger, you can use a jug and/or a set of spoons for measuring out the required quantities. The measurements can be in single (25ml/1fl oz) or double (50ml/2fl oz) bar measures. Do not switch from one type of measurement to another within the same recipe.

Blender or liquidizer

Goblet blenders are the best shape for mixing cocktails that need to be aerated, as well as for creating frothy cocktails or ones made with finely crushed ice. Attempting to break up whole ice cubes in the blender may very well blunt the blades. Opt for an ice bag or dish towel, a rolling pin and plenty of brute force, or better still, use an ice crusher.

Ice bags

These plastic bags that can be filled with water and frozen are a kind of disposable ice tray. You simply press each piece of ice out of them, tearing through the plastic as you go. They also have the advantage of making more rounded pieces of ice, as opposed to the hard-angled cubes that some ice trays produce.

Ice crusher

If the prospect of breaking up ice with a hammer and dish towel comes to seem almost as much of a penance as working on a chain gang, an ice-crushing machine is the answer. It comes in two parts. You fill the top with whole ice cubes, put the lid on and, while

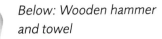

Below: Wooden hammer and towel

pressing down on the top, turn the gramophone-type handle on the side. Take the top half off to retrieve the crystals of ice "snow" from the lower part. Crushed ice is used to fill the glasses for drinks that are to be served frappé. It naturally melts very quickly, though, compared to cubes.

Wooden hammer

Use a wooden hammer for crushing ice. The end of a wooden rolling pin works just as well.

Towel or ice bag

A towel or bag is essential for holding ice cubes when crushing, whether you are creating roughly cracked lumps or a fine snow. It must be scrupulously clean.

Ice bucket and chiller bucket

An ice bucket is useful if you are going to be making several cocktails in quick succession. They are not completely hermetic though, and ice will eventually melt in them, albeit a little more slowly than if left at room temperature. It should not be confused with a chiller bucket for bottles of champagne and white wine, which is bigger and has handles on the sides, but doesn't have a lid. A chiller bucket is intended to be filled with iced water, as opposed to ice alone.

Below: Ice crusher

Mixing pitcher or bar glass

It is useful to have a container in which to mix and stir drinks that are not shaken. The pitcher or bar glass should be large enough to hold two or three drinks. This vessel is intended for drinks that are meant to be clear, not cloudy.

Bar spoon

These long-handled spoons can reach to the bottom of the tallest tumblers and are used in pitchers, or for mixing the drink directly in the glass. Some varieties of bar

Above: Bar spoon, muddlers and corkscrew

Left: Mixing pitcher

spoon look like a large swizzle-stick, with a long spiral-shaped handle and a disc at one end.

Muddler

A long stick with a bulbous end, the muddler is used for crushing sugar or mint leaves, and so is particularly useful when creating juleps or smashes. A variety of sizes is available. It should be used like a pestle in a mixing pitcher; the smaller version is for use in an individual glass. At a pinch, a flattish spoon can be used instead

of a muddler, but then you will find it more awkward to apply sideways rather than downward pressure when trying to press those mint leaves.

Strainer

Used for pouring drinks from a shaker or mixing pitcher into a cocktail glass, the strainer's function is to remove the ice with which the drink has been prepared. Some drinks are served with the ice in (or "on the rocks") but most aren't, the reason being that you don't want the ice to unhelpfully dilute the drink. The best strainer, known professionally as a Hawthorn strainer, is made from stainless steel and looks like a flat spoon with holes and a curl of wire on the underside. It is held over the top of the glass to keep the ice and any other solid ingredients back.

Corkscrew

The fold-up type of corkscrew is known as the Waiter's Friend, and incorporates a can opener and bottle-top flipper as well as the screw itself. It is the most useful version to have to hand as it suits all purposes. The spin-handled corkscrew with a blade for cutting foil is the best one for opening fine wines.

*Above: Nutmeg
grater, zester and cannelle knife*

Sharp knife and squeezer

Citrus fruit is essential in countless cocktails. A good quality, sharp knife is required for halving the fruit, and the squeezer for extracting its juice. Although fruit juice presses are quicker to use, they are more expensive and more boring to wash up afterwards.

Nutmeg grater

A tiny grater with small holes is useful for grating nutmeg over eggnogs, frothy and creamy drinks. If this sounds too fiddly, buy ready-ground nutmeg instead.

Zester and cannelle knife

These are used for presenting fruit attractively to garnish glasses. If you don't already have them, don't feel obliged to run out and buy them, since drinks can look equally attractive with simply sliced fruit. The zester has a row of tiny holes that remove the top layer of skin off a citrus fruit when dragged across it (although the finest gauge on your multi-purpose grater was also designed for just this job).

A cannelle knife (from the French word for a "channel" or "groove") is for making decorative stripes in the skins of a whole fruit. When sliced, they then have a groovy-looking serrated edge. It is, in effect, a narrow-gauged version of a traditional potato peeler, but is purely for decorative purposes.

Egg whisk

Use a whisk to beat a little frothy texture into egg white before you add it to the shaker. It helps the texture of the finished drink no end. An ordinary balloon whisk will do the trick, although for culinary uses, a rotary whisk with a handle (or the electric specimen) is best.

Right: Cocktail sticks and swizzle-sticks

Cocktail sticks and swizzle-sticks

Cocktail sticks (toothpicks) are mainly decorative, used for holding ingredients such as olives that would otherwise sink to the bottom of the glass. And if you intend to eat the olive, it's handier if it's already speared, so that you don't have to commit the appalling faux pas of dipping a finger into the drink to catch it. A swizzle-stick is useful for stirring a drink, and may be substituted by food items such as a stick of celery or cinnamon.

The right glass

Brandy balloon   *Tumbler or rocks glass*

To ensure that glasses are sparkling clean, they should always be washed and dried with a special glass cloth. Although some recipes suggest using chilled glasses, don't put your best crystal in the freezer; leave it at the back of the refrigerator instead. An hour should be enough.

Cocktail or Martini glass
This elegant glass is a wide conical bowl on a tall stem: a design that keeps cocktails cool by keeping warm hands away from the drink. It is by far the most widely used glass, so a set is essential. The design belies the fact that the capacity of this glass is relatively small (about three standard measures). Uses: Rob Roy, Canadian Cocktail, Millionaire, and almost any short, sharp, strong cocktail, including creamy ones.

Collins glass
The tallest of the tumblers, narrow with perfectly straight sides, a Collins glass holds about 350ml/ 12fl oz, and is usually used for serving long drinks made with fresh juices or finished with a sparkling mixer such as soda. This glass can also stand in as the highball glass, which is traditionally slightly less tall. Uses: Blizzard, and all drinks that are to be "topped up" with anything.

Brandy balloon
The brandy glass is designed to trap the fragrance of the drink in the bowl of the glass. Cupping the glass in the palm of the hand further helps to warm it gently and release its aromas. No longer considered the thing to use for best cognac, it nonetheless makes a good cocktail glass for certain short, strong drinks that have been stirred rather than shaken. The wide bowl makes it suitable for drinks with solids floating in them. Uses: Mint Julep.

Tumbler or rocks glass
Classic, short whisky tumblers are used for shorter drinks, served on the rocks, and generally for drinks that are stirred rather than shaken.

Cocktail or Martini glass   *Collins glass*

They should hold about 250ml/ 8fl oz. Uses: Whisky Sour, Old-Fashioned and Rusty Nail.

Large cocktail goblet

Available in various sizes and shapes, large cocktail goblets are good for serving larger frothy drinks, or drinks containing puréed fruit or coconut cream. The wider rim of this type of glass leaves plenty of room for flamboyant and colourful decorations. Uses: Pink Almond.

Champagne saucer

The old-fashioned saucer glass may be frowned on now for champagne, but it is an attractive and elegant design and can be used for a number of cocktails, particularly those that have cracked ice floating in them. Because of the wider surface area, there is plenty of scope for fruity garnishes too. Uses: Perfect Manhattan.

Wine glass

When drinking cold drinks, a long-stemmed, medium-sized glass of about 250ml/8fl oz capacity should be held by the stem so as not to warm the chilled wine or cocktail with the heat of the hand. Uses: Boston, and any short wine cocktails such as spritzers and wine-based punches.

Large cocktail goblet   *Champagne saucer*   *Wine glass*

Bartending know-how

Even clean glasses should be rinsed out and wiped before use, because glasses that have been stored for any length of time can acquire a dusty taste.

Presentation is important – elegant cocktail glasses look even better when served with clean, white linen cloths.

Tricks of the trade

It is worth mastering the techniques for the preparation of good-looking drinks. The following pages give you precise directions for some of the essential procedures, such as crushing ice, as well as some not-so-essential skills, such as making decorative ice cubes. Learning these tricks of the trade is what will distinguish the dedicated bartender from the amateur dabbler.

Crushing ice

Some cocktails require cracked or crushed ice for adding to glasses, or a finely crushed ice "snow" for blending. It isn't a good idea to break ice up in a blender or food processor as you may find it damages the blades. Instead:

1 Lay out a cloth, such as a clean glass cloth or dish towel, on a work surface, and cover half of it with ice cubes. (If you wish, you can also use a cloth ice bag.)

2 Fold the cloth over and, using a rolling pin or mallet, smash down on the ice firmly several times, until you achieve the required fineness.

3 Spoon the ice into glasses or a pitcher. Fine ice snow must be used immediately because it melts, but cracked or roughly crushed ice can be stored in the freezer in plastic bags.

Bartending know-how
For a moderate-sized social gathering, you may have to stay up all night with a sledgehammer. Alternatively, just buy an ice crusher.

Shaking cocktails

Cocktails that contain sugar syrups or creams require more than just a stir; they are combined and chilled with a brief shake. Remember that it is possible to shake only one or two servings at once, so you may have to work quickly in batches. Always use fresh ice each time.

1 Add four or five ice cubes to the shaker and pour in all the ingredients.

2 Put the lid on the shaker. Hold the shaker firmly in one hand, keeping the lid in place with the other hand.

3 Shake vigorously for about 15 seconds to blend simple concoctions, and for 20–30 seconds for drinks with sugar syrups or cream. The shaker should feel extremely cold.

4 Remove the small cap and pour into the prepared glass, using a strainer if the shaker is not already fitted with one.

Bartending know-how
Never shake anything sparkling. This will flatten it.

Making decorative ice cubes

Colourful and imaginatively decorated ice cubes can instantly jolly up the simplest of cocktails. As well as adding fruit, leaves or flowers, you can flavour and colour the water with fruit juices or bitters, and freeze in three stages.

1 Half-fill each compartment of an ice cube tray with water and place in the freezer for 2–3 hours.

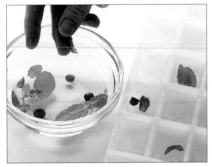

2 Prepare any colourful and decorative ingredients you like – for example, fruit, olives, mint leaves, lemon rind, raisins or borage flowers – and dip each briefly in water. Place in the ice-cube trays, put in the freezer and freeze again.

3 Top up the ice-cube trays with water and return to the freezer to freeze completely. Use as required, but only in one drink per session.

Frosting glasses

The appearance and taste of a cocktail are enhanced if the rim of your glass is frosted. After frosting, place the glass in the refrigerator to chill until needed.

1 Hold the glass upside down, so the juice does not run down the glass. Rub the rim with the cut surface of a lemon, lime, orange or even a slice of fresh pineapple.

2 Keeping the glass upside down, dip the rim into a shallow layer of sugar, coconut or salt. Redip the glass, if necessary, and turn it so that the rim is well-coated.

3 Stand the glass upright and let it sit until the sugar, coconut or salt has dried on the rim, then chill.

The Cocktails

Whisky and Water

The finest whiskies are not necessarily drunk neat. It is widely believed that taming some of the spirit's fire helps to bring up the array of complicated scents and flavours. A dose of water should be added, ideally the same spring water that goes into the whisky itself, otherwise any pure, non-chlorinated water. Half-and-half are the preferred proportions in Scotland and Ireland, while in Tennessee and Kentucky they add a little less than half water to whisky.

1 measure/1¹/₂ tbsp whisky
1 measure/1¹/₂ tbsp water

Pour the ingredients into a tumbler or rocks glass, and swirl to mix.

Whisky on the Rocks

A Scots drinker normally eschews ice in their whisky, however in the States they cram the tumbler full. "On the rocks" means ice but no water.

1 measure/1¹/₂ tbsp whisky

Put as much ice as you prefer into a rocks glass, and add the whisky.

Whisky and Soda

Whiskies go well with soda for those who prefer a friskier drink, and to some extent with ginger ale (especially those fruity Canadian spirits). They should always be iced.

*1 measure/1½ tbsp whisky
soda water, to top up*

Pour the whisky over ice in a rocks glass, and top with soda (or ginger ale) to taste.

Southern Comfort

Like other fine American whiskeys, the whiskey-based liqueur Southern Comfort is intended to be meditatively sipped, but you could try taming its fire and emphasizing its fruitiness with a mixer of orange juice. It's also good with peach nectar on the rocks.

*1 measure/1½ tbsp Southern
    Comfort
2 measures/3 tbsp pressed
    orange juice*

Pour over ice in a tumbler, and stir briefly to mix.

Perfect Manhattan

When making Manhattans it's a matter of preference whether you use sweet vermouth, dry vermouth or a mixture of the two. Both of the former require a dash of Angostura bitters. The last, given here, is such a harmoniously balanced mixture that it doesn't need it.

2 measures/3 tbsp rye whiskey
¼ measure/1 tsp dry vermouth
¼ measure/1 tsp sweet
  red vermouth

Bartending know-how
The favourite Manhattan has come to be equal measures of American or Canadian whiskey and sweet red Italian vermouth, mixed over ice in a large glass, with perhaps a dash of Angostura but certainly with that indispensable cocktail cherry popped in. A dry Manhattan uses dry French vermouth instead of sweet. The accepted compromise is to make up the vermouth quotient with 50% of each.

1 Pour the whiskey and vermouths into a bar glass half-full of ice. Stir well for 30 seconds to mix and chill.

2 Strain on the rocks or straight up into a chilled champagne saucer.

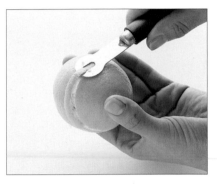

3 Pare away a small strip of lemon rind. Tie it into a knot to help release the oils from the rind, and drop it into the cocktail.

4 Add a maraschino cherry with its stalk intact. As any Manhattan drinker will tell you, the cherry is essential.

Bobby Burns

Similar to Rob Roy, but with the herbal tang of Bénédictine coming through it, this is a drink named after Scotland's national poet. It is best served on Burns Night, January 25.

1½ measures/6 tsp Scotch
¾ measure/3 tsp sweet
   red vermouth
¼ measure/1 tsp Bénédictine

Stir all the ingredients well with ice, and strain into a chilled cocktail glass. Squeeze a spray of oil from a piece of lemon rind over the surface, but in this case don't add the rind to the drink. In the 1920s, the cocktail was shaken, but it seems to work better stirred, which gives a less cloudy result.

Rob Roy

A further modification of the Perfect Manhattan recipe, Rob Roy is made with Scotch, and inclines very much to the sweeter end of the spectrum. It has traditionally been drunk on St Andrew's Day, November 30, but may with confidence be drunk all year round now.

1 measure/1½ tbsp Scotch
1 measure/1½ tbsp sweet
   red vermouth

Shake the ingredients well with ice, and strain into a cocktail glass. Some recipes add a dash of Angostura bitters to the mix as well.

Old-Fashioned

This modified bourbon or rye whiskey has quickly established itself as an all-time classic. Rye results in a thicker, heavier-tasting whiskey with a rather more rustic appeal than bourbon. The cocktail is usually heavily garnished, and served in a particular kind of squat tumbler that is named after the drink.

1/4 measure/1 tsp sugar syrup
2 dashes Angostura bitters
2 measures/3 tbsp bourbon
   or rye whiskey

Mix the sugar and Angostura in an Old-Fashioned glass until the sugar is dissolved. Add plenty of cracked ice and then the whiskey. Throw in a twist of lemon rind, a slice of orange cut laterally from the fruit and a cocktail cherry, and serve with a stirring implement in it. This is the most old-fashioned formula for an Old-Fashioned.

Mint Julep

One of the oldest cocktails of them all, this originated in the southern states of the USA, probably in the 18th century. It's the traditional drink at the Kentucky Derby, the first Saturday in May, and is an incomparably refreshing mixture that has deservedly become a classic.

15ml/1 tbsp caster
   (superfine) sugar
8–10 fresh mint leaves
2/3 measure/1 tbsp hot water
2 measures/3 tbsp bourbon

1 Place the sugar in a mortar or bar glass. Tear the mint leaves into small pieces and add them to the sugar.

2 Bruise them with a pestle or use a muddler to release their flavour and colour.

4 Spoon into a brandy balloon or highball glass and half-fill with crushed ice. Add the bourbon.

3 Add the hot water and grind well together.

5 Stir until the outside of the glass has frosted. Allow to stand for a couple of minutes until the ice melts slightly and dilutes the drink.

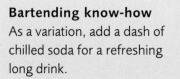

Bartending know-how
As a variation, add a dash of chilled soda for a refreshing long drink.

New York

Despite its name, this simple preparation was first made in the 1920s with Canadian whisky. Scotch can also be used successfully, as can, seemingly, anything but American whiskey.

2 measures/3 tbsp Canadian
   whisky or Scotch
5ml/1 tsp caster (superfine) sugar
juice of half a lime
dash grenadine

Stir all the ingredients vigorously with ice in a pitcher, and then strain into a chilled cocktail glass. Squeeze a twist of lemon over the drink, but don't drop it in.

Canada Cocktail

An engagingly sweet and fruity cocktail that obviously has to be made with whisky from Canada. Canadian Club is a fine brand, and is generally available.

1¹/₂ measures/6 tsp
   Canadian whisky
¹/₄ measure/1 tsp Cointreau
2 dashes Angostura bitters
5ml/1 tsp caster (superfine) sugar

Shake all the ingredients well with ice, and strain into a cocktail glass. Garnish with a twist of orange rind.

Whisky Mac

The classic cold remedy is half-and-half good Scotch and green ginger wine (preferably Crabbie's). These days, it is generally served over ice in a rocks glass, but traditionally it was taken straight up. Whether it actually gets rid of a cold must be open to doubt, but it certainly makes you feel better.

1 measure/1½ tbsp Scotch
1 measure/1½ tbsp green
*   ginger wine*

Pour the ingredients into a rocks glass, with or without ice.

Whisky Sour

American whiskeys are best for this preparation. Some people add a brief squirt of soda. If you find this formula a little too sour, add a little more sugar.

juice of half a lemon
5ml/1 tsp caster (superfine) sugar
generous 1 measure/1½ tbsp
* whiskey*
dash soda water (optional)

Mix the lemon juice and sugar in a small tumbler with two or three cubes of ice. When the sugar is dissolved, add a generous measure of whiskey and stir again.

Millionaire

Several cocktails have been recorded over the years under this name. The Savoy Cocktail Book lists two alternatives, one based on rum, the other on gin. This one is from roughly the same era, though.

1¹/₂ measures/6 tsp bourbon
³/₄ measure/3 tsp Cointreau
dash grenadine
¹/₂ egg white

Shake all the ingredients well with ice, and strain into a cocktail glass. Garnish with a half-slice of lemon.

Buckaroo

Not many cocktails work well with cola, but this is an honourable exception. The pronounced bitter note contributed by the Angostura is essential and should not be omitted.

1¹/₂ measures/6 tsp bourbon
2.5ml/¹/₂ tsp Angostura bitters
5 measures/120ml/4fl oz
   Coca-Cola

Add the first two ingredients to a highball glass containing plenty of cracked ice. Stir briskly and then top up with cola. Serve with a swizzle-stick for further stirring.

Rusty Nail

A short, sharp drink, this is a classic half-and-half recipe made with Scotch and Drambuie. It manages to do perfect justice to both ingredients. When served without ice, it is known as a Straight Up Nail.

1¹/₂ measures/6 tsp Scotch
1¹/₂ measures/6 tsp Drambuie

Pour both ingredients over crushed ice in a rocks glass or whisky tumbler, and stir gently. No garnish is necessary. Some prefer to leave the ice cubes whole so as not to dilute the drink too much. It should be drunk quickly.

Bartending know-how
A Rusty Nail is a Drambuie cocktail. Attempts to make this fine Scottish liqueur blend with anything other than Scotch always seem to come to grief.

Sea Dog

This is a long Scotch whisky drink with a citrus twist. Despite the presence of two types of alcohol, it should end up tasting deceptively innocuous. For a sweeter drink, add a second sugar cube.

1–2 sugar cubes
2 dashes Angostura bitters
2 orange wedges
2 lemon wedges
²/₃ measure/1 tbsp Scotch
1 measure/1¹/₂ tbsp Bénédictine
2 measures/3 tbsp soda water, chilled

Put the sugar cube at the bottom of a highball glass, add the bitters and allow to soak into the sugar cube. Add the orange and lemon wedges and, using a muddler, press the juices from the fruit. Fill the glass with cracked ice. Add the whisky and Bénédictine, and mix together well with a swizzle-stick. Add the chilled soda water. Serve with the muddler and a maraschino cherry.

Gall Bracer

Short and smart, this drink is served on the rocks in a tumbler, or in a long-stemmed glass with a maraschino cherry. Angostura bitters make a particularly good combination with American whiskeys, emphasizing their woody notes, while the grenadine gently mitigates any excess bitterness.

2 dashes Angostura bitters
2 dashes grenadine
2 measures/3 tbsp bourbon
*   or rye whiskey*

1 Half-fill a bar glass with ice cubes. Add the Angostura bitters, grenadine and whiskey, and stir well to chill.

3 Squeeze lemon rind over the top and then discard.

2 Place some ice in a small tumbler and pour the cocktail over it.

4 Garnish with a cherry, if desired. For a longer drink, finish with soda or sparkling mineral water.

Bunny Hug

This drink was named after a popular ragtime dance of the 1910s, and was originally banned in some states of America. It is not a concoction for the novice cocktail drinker.

1 measure/1¹/₂ tbsp Scotch
1 measure/1¹/₂ tbsp gin
1 measure/1¹/₂ tbsp pastis

Shake all the ingredients together with ice, and strain into a cocktail glass.

Modern Cocktail

The meaning of "modern" here is not as in 21st century, but as in 1920s. There were two cocktails with this name even then. One had whisky and sloe gin in it, but this seems to have been the original. It has a strong and unusual flavour that is an acquired taste, but one that you may well find yourself acquiring.

2 measures/3 tbsp Scotch
1/3 measure/1 1/2 tsp dark rum
1/4 measure/1 tsp absinthe
1/4 measure/1 tsp orange bitters
   (or curaçao)
1/3 measure/1 1/2 tsp lemon juice

Shake all the ingredients well with ice, and strain into a cocktail glass. Garnish with a twist of lemon.

Brainstorm

Here is a recipe that specifically calls for Irish whiskey. Its smooth, triple-distilled flavour works exceptionally well with the other ingredients. Jameson's would be a particularly good brand to use.

2 measures/3 tbsp Irish whiskey
2 dashes dry vermouth
2 dashes Bénédictine

Half-fill an Old-Fashioned glass with cracked ice, and then add the ingredients in this order. Stir gently, add a twist of orange rind, and serve with a swizzle-stick for stirring.

Loch Lomond

This is another very simple treatment for Scotch for those who are not quite up to taking it neat.

1½ measures/6 tsp Scotch
¼ measure/1 tsp sugar syrup
2 dashes Angostura bitters

Shake all the ingredients well with ice, and strain into a cocktail glass. Squeeze a piece of lemon over the surface and discard.

Bartending know-how
When Scotch is given as few additives as it is in the Loch Lomond cocktail, be as choosy as any whisky connoisseur about which type you use.

Duck Soup

A fruity preparation in which bourbon is given the treatment more normally accorded to rum. It works well, though, showing what a versatile drink American whiskey is.

2 measures/3 tbsp bourbon
1/2 measure/2 tsp apricot brandy
3/4 measure/3 tsp lemon juice
3/4 measure/3 tsp pineapple juice
5ml/1 tsp caster (superfine) sugar

Shake all the ingredients well with ice, and strain into a rocks glass that is half-filled with cracked ice. Garnish with a slice of lemon and a cherry.

Churchill

The British wartime leader is well-served by having this sophisticated and powerful cocktail named after him, even though Scotch wasn't his favourite tipple.

1½ measures/6 tsp Scotch
½ measure/2 tsp sweet
  red vermouth
½ measure/2 tsp Cointreau
½ measure/2 tsp lime juice

Shake all the ingredients well with ice, and strain into a chilled cocktail glass. Garnish with a half-slice of orange and a slice of lime.

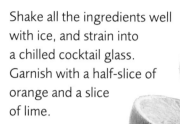

Plank Walker

Another recipe that puns on a famous name, this one being the celebrated Scotch brand, Johnnie Walker. It's a hardcore, all-alcohol mixture.

1½ measures/6 tsp Johnnie
  Walker Red Label Scotch
½ measure/2 tsp sweet
  red vermouth
½ measure/2 tsp yellow
  Chartreuse

Shake all the ingredients well with ice, and strain into a rocks glass half-filled with roughly cracked ice. Add a wedge of lemon.

Jack Frost

The Jack in the name refers to the ever-popular Tennessee whiskey brand, Jack Daniel's, and so that is the type that must be used. This is an exotic and highly appealing cocktail.

1 measure/1¹/₂ tbsp Jack Daniel's
³/₄ measure/3 tsp dry vermouth
¹/₃ measure/1¹/₂ tsp crème
    de banane
1 measure/1¹/₂ tbsp passion
    fruit juice
¹/₃ measure/1¹/₂ tsp pineapple
    juice

Shake all the ingredients well with ice, and strain into a large cocktail glass that has been half-filled with crushed ice. The drink could be garnished with a slice of lemon on a stick with a chunk of juicy, ripe pineapple.

Kentucky Kernel

The geographical reference of this drink indicates that it's a bourbon cocktail, and the second half of the name refers to the apricot kernels from which its other alcoholic ingredient is made. Together, they combine to make an appealing fruity and sweet cocktail, and the grapefruit juice brings it all into focus.

1¹/₂ measures/6 tsp bourbon
¹/₂ measure/2 tsp apricot brandy
1 measure/1¹/₂ tbsp grapefruit juice
¹/₄ measure/1 tsp grenadine

Shake all the ingredients well with ice, and pour the drink – ice and all – into a rocks glass.

Pamplemousse

The name is the French word for "grapefruit", so it's not hard to work out what the principal flavour of this cocktail should be. Grapefruit juice has a very astringent effect on the tastebuds, so it is generally necessary to throw it into relief in a cocktail recipe with sweeter, gentler flavours, hence the pineapple.

1½ measures/6 tsp Canadian
   whisky
½ measure/2 tsp Southern
   Comfort
2 measures/3 tbsp grapefruit juice
¼ measure/1 tsp pineapple syrup

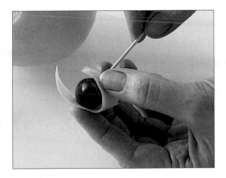

Shake all the ingredients well with ice, and then strain into a rocks glass half-filled with cracked ice. Add a short twist of grapefruit rind and a cocktail cherry.

Artists' Special

This drink is so-named because it was invented at the Artists' Club in the rue Pigalle, Paris, in the 1920s. The red ingredient was originally redcurrant syrup, but grenadine can be used to perfectly good effect instead. The mixture of Scotch and sweet sherry at its heart is a very appealing one.

1 measure/1¹⁄₂ tbsp Scotch
*1 measure/1¹⁄₂ tbsp sweet
   brown sherry*
¹⁄₂ measure/2 tsp lemon juice
¹⁄₂ measure/2 tsp grenadine

Shake all the ingredients well with ice, and strain into a cocktail glass. Add a half-slice of lemon.

Pleasant Dreams

This fruity treatment for bourbon would make a very comforting nightcap – so long as you confine yourself to just the one, that is.

1½ measures/6 tsp bourbon
¾ measure/3 tsp crème de mûre
½ measure/2 tsp peach schnapps

Shake all the ingredients well with ice, and pour without straining into a chilled rocks glass.

Algonquin

This is named after the elegant New York hotel where Dorothy Parker once ruled the roost. The types of whisky to be used are once again quite specific.

2 measures/3 tbsp rye or
* Canadian whisky*
1 measure/1½ tbsp dry vermouth
1 measure/1½ tbsp pineapple
* juice*

Shake all the ingredients well with ice, and strain into a rocks glass half-filled with cracked ice. Garnish with lemon.

Tivoli

There is an Italian connection in this powerful little cocktail to reflect its name, but it actually comes by way of Scandinavia and Kentucky.

1½ measures/6 tsp bourbon
½ measure/2 tsp sweet
*   red vermouth*
½ measure/2 tsp aquavit
dash Campari

Shake all the ingredients well with ice, and strain into a chilled cocktail glass. Garnish the drink with a half-slice of lemon.

Grenoble

This is a superbly fruity cocktail with quite a kick, and one that demonstrates what a good mixer Kentucky whiskey is.

1½ measures/6 tsp bourbon
½ measure/2 tsp crème
*   de framboise*
½ measure/2 tsp Cointreau
1 measure/1½ tbsp orange juice
¼ measure/1 tsp orgeat syrup

Shake all the ingredients well with ice, and strain into a cocktail glass. Garnish with a half-slice of orange and a raspberry skewered on a cocktail stick.

Blizzard

The trick with this drink is to shake it for longer than normal with masses of ice until the mixture is extremely frosty-looking. That, incidentally, goes some way to disguise the high proportion of bourbon in it.

3 measures/4$^1/_2$ tbsp bourbon
1 measure/1$^1/_2$ tbsp cranberry juice
$^2/_3$ measure/1 tbsp lemon juice
30ml/2 tbsp sugar syrup

Shake all the ingredients extremely well with plenty of large ice cubes, and pour the mixture unstrained into a chilled highball glass. Garnish with a couple of cranberries and perhaps a slice of lemon.

Rocky Mountain

Here is another of those cocktails that calls for three specific brands, and wouldn't be quite the same with substitutes. Be sure to follow the specified proportions carefully, in order to arrive at the precise balance of complex flavours in the drink. Its light, delicately herbal tinge is very attractive.

1¹/₂ measures/6 tsp Canadian Club
¹/₂ measure/2 tsp Glayva
¹/₄ measure/1 tsp Punt e Mes

Shake all the ingredients well with ice, and pour without straining into a chilled rocks glass.

Bartending know-how
The Italian aperitif Punt e Mes, created in Turin in 1870, contains around four dozen herbs and spices on a white wine base. In Italy, it is traditionally accompanied by a piece of strong, dark chocolate.

Paddy

Another traditional one, this was originally made with the Irish whiskey brand of the same name. In the 1920s, it had equal quantities of whiskey and vermouth and slightly less Angostura, which would obviously make for a sweeter result. This is today's drier and more sophisticated formula.

1¹/₂ measures/6 tsp Irish whiskey
³/₄ measure/3 tsp sweet
   red vermouth
3 dashes Angostura bitters

Shake all the ingredients well with ice, and strain into a chilled cocktail glass. Garnish with a quarter-slice of lemon.

Highland Morning

Although the name seems to be encouraging you to drink one of these for breakfast, a little later in the day might be wiser.

1 measure/1½ tbsp Scotch
¾ measure/3 tsp Cointreau
3 measures/4½ tbsp
*   grapefruit juice*

Shake all the ingredients well with ice, and pour (unstrained if you really are having it in the morning) into a chilled rocks glass. The drink could be garnished with a twist of grapefruit rind and perhaps a half-slice of orange to reflect the presence of Cointreau in the mix.

Loch Ness

Named after the famous yet elusive monster claimed to inhabit Loch Ness, this Scottish cocktail is a tough cookie. The recipe dates from the 1920s.

1½ measures/6 tsp Scotch
1 measure/1½ tbsp Pernod
¼ measure/1 tsp sweet
   red vermouth

Shake all the ingredients well with ice, and pour without straining into a chilled rocks glass or Old-Fashioned glass. Do not garnish.

Tipperary

You'll certainly know you've had one of these! Tipperary is an old 1920s mixture that's all alcohol, and packs the considerable punch of Chartreuse. If you're feeling brave, the Chartreuse was originally a whole measure too.

1 measure/1½ tbsp Irish whiskey
1 measure/1½ tbsp sweet
   red vermouth
½ measure/2 tsp green Chartreuse

Add the ingredients to a pitcher with plenty of cracked ice, and stir until cold enough to frost the sides of the glass. Strain into a pre-chilled cocktail glass.

Saracen

The name of this drink refers to the story of the Saracen's head once depicted on the label of the Scotch-based liqueur Glayva, in commemoration of the teenage warrior who carried Robert the Bruce's heart back to Scotland, along with the head of an enemy fighter impaled on a lance, after the king's defeat at the hands of the Saracen armies. This is a very dry cocktail that makes a wonderfully effective aperitif.

1 measure/1½ tbsp Scotch
½ measure/2 tsp Glayva
½ measure/2 tsp pale dry sherry
dash orange bitters (or curaçao)
1 measure/1½ tbsp soda water

Shake the Scotch, Glayva, dry sherry and orange bitters with ice, and pour without straining into a tumbler. Add the soda. Decorate with a piece of orange rind.

Southern Peach

The peach notes in the classic whiskey liqueur of the southern States are accentuated by its being mixed with a sweet liqueur of the same flavour in this cream cocktail. Notwithstanding that, this is one of the more grown-up cream drinks. It isn't as straightforwardly sweet and milkshakey as many another cream concoction, but has a bracing southern twang to it, emphasized by the splash of Angostura.

1 measure/1½ tbsp
   Southern Comfort
1 measure/1½ tbsp peach brandy
1 measure/1½ tbsp double
   (heavy) cream
dash Angostura bitters

Shake all the ingredients well with plenty of ice, and strain into a tumbler. Garnish with wedges of ripe peach.

Pink Almond

The colour of this isn't actually pink, more a sort of off-puce, but the flavour is indubitably of almond, so at least half the name is right.

1 measure/1½ tbsp Scotch
½ measure/2 tsp crème de noyau
½ measure/2 tsp kirsch
½ measure/2 tsp lemon juice
½ measure/2 tsp orgeat syrup

Shake all the ingredients well with ice, and strain into a wine goblet. Garnish with a twist of lemon and two or three slivers of flaked almond.

Casanova

Named after the famous 18th-century Italian womanizer, this cream cocktail gives a kick that can be enjoyed by men and women alike.

1 measure/1½ tbsp bourbon
½ measure/2 tsp dolce (sweet)
   Marsala
½ measure/2 tsp Kahlúa
1 measure/1½ tbsp double
   (heavy) cream

Shake all the ingredients with plenty of ice. Strain into a cocktail glass and sprinkle with ground nutmeg.

Boston

This is one of those drinks that contains raw egg. Use only a very fresh, free-range egg if you're going to take the plunge. Although there is a pinch of sugar in it, the underlying mixture is quite dry.

$1^1/_2$ measures/6 tsp bourbon
$1^1/_2$ measures/6 tsp sercial
   (dry) Madeira
2.5ml/$^1/_2$ tsp caster (superfine)
   sugar
1 egg yolk

Shake all the ingredients together with ice. Strain into a small wine glass and sprinkle with grated nutmeg.

Highland Milk Punch

This is just the sort of thing to keep the cold at bay on frosty nights in the frozen north, or anywhere else for that matter.

2 measures/3 tbsp Scotch
1 measure/1½ tbsp Drambuie
1 egg, beaten
250ml/8fl oz full-cream
    (whole) milk

Put all the ingredients into a small pan and heat gently, stirring all the time to incorporate the egg and prevent the milk from burning on the bottom of the pan. Just before the mixture boils, pour it into a mug and sprinkle the surface of the drink with powdered cinnamon.

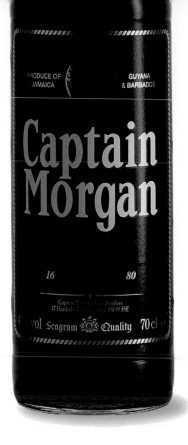

Jamaica Shake

Combining the best of both worlds, this cream cocktail brings together the complementary richnesses of American whiskey and Jamaican rum. It's really a milkshake for adults.

1¹/₂ measures/6 tsp bourbon
1 measure/1¹/₂ tbsp dark
    Jamaican rum
1 measure/1¹/₂ tbsp double
    (heavy) cream

Shake all the ingredients well with ice to amalgamate the cream, and strain into a cocktail glass. Sprinkle grated chocolate over the top.

Ring of Kerry

Irish whiskey lends itself beautifully to all sorts of creamy treatments, and in this cocktail it appears with its much-loved compatriot, Bailey's Irish Cream.

1¹/₂ measures/6 tsp Irish whiskey
1 measure/1¹/₂ tbsp
    Bailey's Irish Cream
¹/₂ measure/2 tsp Kahlúa

Shake all the ingredients well with ice, and strain into a chilled cocktail glass. Sprinkle 5ml/1 tsp grated chocolate over the top.

Coffee Eggnog

This is a rather special coffee drink, particularly suitable for daytime summer-holiday festivities. It's worth making in bulk for an outdoor occasion, and this recipe serves six to eight.

8 eggs, separated
225g/8oz sugar
250ml/8fl oz cold strong coffee
(espresso strength or
filter/cafetière brewed at
75g/3oz coffee per 1 litre/
1³/₄ pints water)
220ml/7¹/₂fl oz Scotch
or bourbon
220ml/7¹/₂fl oz double
(heavy) cream
120ml/4fl oz whipped cream
ground nutmeg

Thoroughly beat the egg yolks, then add the sugar, mixing well. Heat gently in a pan over a low heat, stirring with a wooden spoon. Allow to cool a few minutes, stir in the coffee and whisky, and then slowly add the cream, stirring well. Beat the egg whites until stiff and stir into the eggnog, mixing well. Pour into small round cups, top each with a small dollop of whipped cream and sprinkle ground nutmeg over the top.

Irish Chocolate Velvet

This is a luxurious creamy hot chocolate drink, with just a touch of alcohol to fortify it. It would be the perfect antidote to a winter morning spent working outdoors. This recipe serves four.

250ml/8fl oz double (heavy) cream
400ml/14fl oz milk
115g/4oz milk chocolate, chopped
   into small pieces
30ml/2 tbsp cocoa powder
60ml/4 tbsp Irish whiskey
whipped cream, for topping

Whip half the cream in a bowl until it is thick enough to hold its shape. Place the milk and chocolate in a pan and heat gently, stirring, until the chocolate has melted. Whisk in the cocoa, then bring to the boil. Remove from the heat and stir in the remaining cream and the Irish whiskey. Pour quickly into four warmed heatproof mugs or glasses and top each serving with a generous spoonful of the whipped cream, finishing with a garnish of milk chocolate curls.

Bartending know-how
This recipe works equally well with Scotch whisky or bourbon.

Index